I0465108

A Girl Named Sandy

The Legal Lessons and Cautionary Tales from the Death of Sandra Bland

By Marion TD Lewis

Library of Congress Cataloguing in Publication Data:
Lewis, M
ISBN:9781522953951
     1.   Non Fiction
A Girl Named Sandy
Printed in the United States of America 10 9 8 7 6 5 4 3 2 1

INTRODUCTION

I can scarcely ever discuss Sandra Bland's story without becoming a little bit emotional. I don't know what it is but her death was a game changer, a Eureka moment for me. It woke me up out of my reverie and carefully constructed cave/wonderland/escapist colony I have been living in and opened my eyes to the fact that our country, and perhaps our world, is in serious crisis in more ways than one.

When I heard about Sandra's story, I finally I had to admit to myself that something is seriously wrong in America with regard to some American citizens and their interactions with law enforcement throughout the country.

These interactions are increasingly deadly for a certain group in the population. It is not that I had not heard of so many similar stories like Sandra's. After all, one can scarcely turn on the news or computer without being bombarded with yet another story.

However, Sandra's story really resonated in a way that many others hadn't. Maybe it is because she looks like someone I could have known whether as a friend, sibling, colleague or neighbour. Indeed, if I may be so honest, she reminded me of myself. I thought, "Oh my god, if that could happen to her, it could happen to me." And this was my epiphany. This is where the music stopped for me and I knew that I had to do something, to be a part of the solution to what I perceive as a very grave problem. I could not continue to remain silent, sweetly cocooned in my perfect little world because this made me a part of the problem. I did not want to be a part of the problem. But what could I do? I have neither power nor resources. I have no influence or Facebook friends. The only thing I could think of was to write this book and to try to focus on the broader implications of her death for us all as Americans, and more broadly, for the human race itself.

Though I am not a practicing attorney, I do have a legal background, and so I thought I would focus more on certain legal points that I believe apply to Sandra's case and other cases like hers. Still, please note that this is not my area of expertise so I am making general points, not offering legal advice.

I intentionally chose to use a story-telling approach because I want this book to be read even by young children and for them to be able to understand the points I try to make. This is the small thing I think I can do to be part of the solution of what has become, in my view, and extremely serious human rights crisis in the United States.

A Girl Named Sandy

Once upon a time a little baby girl was born in Naperville Illinois to a woman named Geneva. Geneva named her bundle of joy Sandra and gave her the middle name Annette. But as the little girl grew, everybody called her "Sandy."

Sandy spent her first few years of life with her mother and sisters in Naperville, a beautiful city in Illinois that traces its roots back to a man named Joseph Naper, a European settler who arrived by schooner across the Great Lakes in 1831. She was a lucky little girl to be born in such a beautiful place.

Naperville was voted one of the most beautiful cities in America, but sadly, Sandy did not live there all her life. Years after she was born, she moved with her family to the town of Villa Park, Illinois, just outside of Chicago.

Villa Park was pretty too, and here, she attended Willowbrook High School named for the weeping willow trees close by. She was a good student who was very active with lots of extra-curricular activities in addition to her studies. She joined the track team and the volleyball team and excelled at both. She was a varsity cheerleader and was a member of the marching band. In high school, Sandy was a very talkative girl who believed in standing up for herself and for others who she thought did not have a voice. Her sisters and friends thought she was very brave.

Sandy thought of herself as a "warrior." Ironically, this was the nickname for her high school at Willowbrook. Sometimes this tendency of thinking she was a warrior got her into a little bit of trouble, and when she was 28 years old, this may have led to her death.

Little Sandy was a pretty girl when she was growing up. She had brown skin, big, bright, brown eyes, and a joyful smile that drew people in. She was one of five sisters all with names that began with "S" sort of the same way as the Kardashian girls' names all begin with "K".

Her sisters Sharon, Shante, Sierra & Shavon were her best friends. They got along very well, sort of like the Kardashians. They liked to have fun and they often dressed alike. They enjoyed spending time together and with their mother, Geneva. In fact, they were known as "Geneva's girls" in their circles.

Sharon and Sandy were particularly close and when Sharon got married, Sandy was her maid of honor. At the wedding, Sandy wore her hair in long beautiful African braids, and she also wore a lovely satin dress. Everybody thought both she and her sister looked like princesses.

Among other things, Sandy was a social activist. She believed in racial justice for all Americans. She was particularly troubled by police brutality against some members of our American society, specifically young black men and women who she felt were disproportionately killed and brutalized while in police custody. And she felt that Blacks did not enjoy equality in American society.

She spoke out about this and often engaged in activism on social networks like Twitter and Facebook to bring awareness to, and fight against, this problem. Sometimes, the things she said made people uncomfortable.

In July 2015, when she was 28 year old, Sandy found a new job at her alma mater in Texas after many months of searching for work. The day she got word that she had been hired, she was ecstatic. She sent her sister Sharon a text message full of excitement about the new job, saying, "I GOT THE JOB!!!" Sharon was very happy for her sister.

Sandy moved from Chicago to Texas to start her new job as a "student ambassador to the alumni association at Prairie View A&M University." She was really looking forward to starting this new chapter in her life but fate would intervene when she was stopped for a minor traffic signalling infraction by a state trooper, days after arriving in Texas.

According to reports based on video footage, this is part of the conversation between Sandy and the trooper:

TROOPER: You seem very irritated.

SANDRA BLAND: I am. I really am, because I feel like it's crap, what I'm getting a ticket for. I was getting out of your way. You were speeding up, tailing me, so I move over, and you stop me. So, yeah, I am a little irritated, but that doesn't stop you from giving me a ticket, so.

TROOPER: Are you done?

SANDRA BLAND: You asked me what was wrong, and I told you.

TROOPER: OK.

SANDRA BLAND: So now I'm done, yeah.

TROOPER: OK. You mind putting out your cigarette, please?

SANDRA BLAND: I'm in my car. Why do I have to put out my cigarette?

TROOPER: Well, you can step on out now.

SANDRA BLAND: I don't have to step out of my car.

TROOPER: Step out of the car.

SANDRA BLAND: Why am I—

TROOPER: Step out of the car.

SANDRA BLAND: No, you don't have—no, you don't have the right—you do not—

TROOPER: Step out of the car!

SANDRA BLAND: You do not have the right to do that.

TROOPER: I do have the right. Now step out, or I will remove you.

JUAN GONZÁLEZ: As the dash cam video continues, [the trooper] escalates the situation when he threatens to "light [Sandra Bland] up."

SANDRA BLAND: Why am I being apprehended? You're trying to give me a ticket for a failure—

TROOPER: I said get out of the car.

SANDRA BLAND: Why am I being apprehended? You just opened my car door.

TROOPER: I'm giving you a lawful order. I am going to drag you out of there.

SANDRA BLAND: You opened my car door. So you're going—you're threatening to drag me out of my own car?

TROOPER: Get out of the car!

SANDRA BLAND: And then you're going to assault me? Wow.

TROOPER: I will light you up! Get out! Now!

SANDRA BLAND: Wow.

TROOPER: Get out of the car!

SANDRA BLAND: Really? For a failure to signal? You're doing all of this for a failure to signal?

TROOPER: Get over there!

SANDRA BLAND: Right, yeah. Yeah, let's take this to court. Let's do it.

TROOPER: Go ahead!

SANDRA BLAND: For a failure to signal. Yeah, for a failure to signal.

TROOPER: Get off the phone!

SANDRA BLAND: On my school.

TROOPER: Get off the phone!

SANDRA BLAND: I'm not on the phone. I have a right to record. This is my property.

TROOPER: Put your phone down.

SANDRA BLAND: This is my property.

TROOPER: Put your phone down!

SANDRA BLAND: Sir?

TROOPER: Put your phone down! Right now! Put your phone down!

SANDRA BLAND: For a [bleep] failure to signal, my goodness.

TROOPER: Come over here!

SANDRA BLAND: Y'all are— y'all are [inaudible].

TROOPER: Come over here now!

SANDRA BLAND: You feeling good about yourself?

TROOPER: Stand right here.

SANDRA BLAND: You feeling good about yourself?

TROOPER: Stand right there.

SANDRA BLAND: For a failure to signal. You feel real good about yourself, don't you?

TROOPER: Turn around. Turn around.

SANDRA BLAND: You feel good about yourself, don't you?

TROOPER=: Turn around now!

SANDRA BLAND: What are you—

31

TROOPER: Put your hands behind your back and turn around.

SANDRA BLAND: Why am I being arrested?

The trooper took Sandy to the local jail where she was detained for three days. On the third day, she was found hanging by a trash bag in her prison cell. The coroner ruled her death a "suicide."

After her death, Sandy's family including her sister Sharon and her Mother Geneva were understandably distraught. Their sister and daughter had died suddenly, unexpectedly and mysteriously while in police custody. Sadly, Sandy was not the only young American to die under similar types of circumstances.

Many Americans of all racial groups and backgrounds joined protests online and marched to bring attention to law enforcement abuses and injustices in our country. Groups like "Black Lives Matter" as well as others joined the protests in Sandy's name, by starting hashtags like #sandrabland, #sayhername and #justiceforsandrabland.

Sandy's race and gender and other qualifying characteristics are tertiary to the fact that she was, first and foremost, a human person and part of our human family. And second, she was AMERICAN, and a unique member of our American family.

Maybe that is why so many Americans were confused about how something like what happened to Sandy could happen in our country to a fellow American just because of her failure to signal properly in traffic.

In America human rights and liberty and freedom underpin everything we are and stand for and many American people feel that Sandy's human rights were infringed when she was arrested for something so minor.

They just can't imagine
something like that happening
to them or members of their
group even though for certain
groups, it seems to happen
routinely.

Sandy did talk back to the police officer who arrested her and she challenged her arrest. Some say that was a big mistake. It certainly was very brave of her but that could be because of who she was: An American.

America is the land of the free and the home of the brave and it is a reputation that she must have taken to heart. In America everyone is equal before the law, no matter who they are. Many lives were sacrificed in our country's history to win this point.

This is why our country and democracy is an example for the rest of the world today. In America, *all* citizens are protected by both their state and the federal constitution which guarantee due process, equal protection and civil rights for all regardless of their race or background.

In America, all citizens are furthermore entitled to freedom from unreasonable searches, seizures and arrests and we are entitled to the protection, not abuse, by law enforcement officials acting under color of law.

These basic rights that all Americans are entitled to and should expect pursuant to the laws of the United States, are also strengthened by international law. Luckily, most Americans enjoy these rights throughout their entire lives. But unfortunately, for some groups in America, there is still a lot of struggle to safeguard these basic rights.

Sandy is lucky that she was born in a country that is not just an example for the rest of the world, but is a member of several international treaties and conventions whose sole purpose is to protect human rights from human rights abuses – anywhere in the world.

These treaties include but are not limited to the *United Nations Charter,* the *Universal Declaration of Human Rights*, and others. In addition to its domestic, state and federal constitution, the United States has signed and ratified the *International Covenant on Civil and Political Rights.*

In this international treaty, made a part of our American law through ratification in 1992, it is provides that:

Each State Party to the present Covenant undertakes:

(a) To ensure that any person whose rights or freedoms as herein recognized are violated shall have an effective remedy, notwithstanding that the violation has been committed by persons acting in an official capacity;

(b) To ensure that any person claiming such a remedy shall have his right thereto determined by competent judicial, administrative or legislative authorities, or by any other competent authority provided for by the legal system of the State, and to *develop the possibilities of judicial remedy*;

(c) To ensure that the competent authorities shall

enforce such remedies when granted.

Indeed, throughout this document, including articles 2(6), 6, 7, 9, 14, 16, 17, 19 and 26, our country agreed to insure that *all* its citizens and persons on American soil would have certain basic protections just by virtue of being human beings.

Article 9 is particularly relevant in Sandy's case because it reads as follows:

Everyone has the right to liberty and security of person. No one shall be subjected to arbitrary arrest or detention. No one shall be deprived of his liberty except on such grounds and in accordance with such procedure as are established by law.

2. Anyone who is arrested shall be informed, at the time of arrest, of the reasons for his arrest and shall be promptly informed of any charges against him.

3. Anyone arrested or detained on a criminal charge shall be brought promptly before a judge or other officer authorized by law to exercise judicial power and shall be entitled to trial within a

reasonable time or to release. It shall not be the general rule that persons awaiting trial shall be detained in custody, but release may be subject to guarantees to appear for trial, at any other stage of the judicial proceedings, and, should occasion arise, for execution of the judgement.

4. Anyone who is deprived of his liberty by arrest or detention shall be entitled to take proceedings before a court, in order that that court may decide without delay on the lawfulness of his detention and order his release if the detention is not lawful.

5. Anyone who has been the victim of unlawful arrest or detention shall have an enforceable right to compensation.

Did Sandy Bland enjoy these rights guaranteed to every American when she died in a jail cell in Texas in 2015? Were the "possibilities for judicial remedies" sufficiently developed as required by international law so as to allow her to attain justice both pre and post-mortem?

It is not clear. In December 2015, a grand jury declined to indict anyone in Sandy's bizarre and mysterious death. Americans will never know what happened to one of America's daughters.

Sandy, the beautiful little American girl from Naperville, Illinois, is the only other person who could tell us what happened and unfortunately she is no longer with us.

It would seem clear however, that if there are laws in our domestic legal system that allows a person's civil right to be abridged in the manner that it appears Sandy's rights were abridged, with what appears to be an arbitrary arrest that ended with her death three days later in a jail cell, that our lawmakers are obliged to further develop our domestic laws in order to bring our laws into strict compliance with international law. In so doing, greater clarity for law enforcement personnel will be achieved with respect to the limits of the exercise of their discretion when arresting persons, with an understanding that, as parties to these international conventions, the United States and its officials, including the police, must do everything in their power to ascertain that the civil and human rights of all citizens are protected. By further developing our domestic penal laws with a view to diminishing the number of cases such as Sandy's case, the legislature will assist law enforcement personnel with doing their jobs in a more efficient way and this will result in a higher level of equality and justice for all Americans.

What does Sandy's death mean for those of us who remain to contemplate it? Does her death matter? Should her death matter? Her death does and should matter to all of us as human persons, and as Americans because she was one of us. She was a part of our human family and our American family. What happened to her could one day happen to someone else.

Even if we happen not to be a member of all the groups to which Sandy belonged, her membership in our American family made her one of us. And her misfortune could one day fall on someone of us, or those we know or love if we fail to take collective action to ameliorate this problem in our penal system and society.

Sandy's arrest and her death in Texas concerns *every* American who believes in the principles proclaimed in the *Charter of the United Nations*, the *Universal Declaration of Human Rights* and the *International Covenant on Civil and Political Rights*, as well as our state and federal constitutions all of which profess the "recognition of the inherent dignity and of the equal and inalienable rights of all members of the human family."

As part of our American family, Sandy's death reminds us of our commitment to "freedom, justice and peace in the world," by virtue of our signature and ratification of these international agreements which vow to recognize basic human rights as having derived from the "inherent dignity of the human person" for every person in the world. Furthermore, as Americans, Sandy's death reminds us that by signing these international agreement our country and its officials acting on our behalf are obligated "under the Charter of the United Nations to promote universal respect for, and observance of, human rights and freedoms."

This is not just lip service. This carries responsibility and challenges to rise to our highest selves, individually and also as a country.

Sandy was a young American activist before her untimely death in 2015. In her memory, Americans must reaffirm our commitment to uphold the values espoused in our laws personally, and hold each other, including those employed to protect us like the police, accountable when anyone of us runs afoul of our duties and obligations under these laws. We must not pretend not to know when there are inequalities and injustices.

This is important for many reasons but probably most urgently because the United States is an example and beacon of freedom and human rights for the rest of the world to follow. Being an example is an action, not just an ideal. It is earned, not taken. To *be* an example, we must *set* the example first – at home and make sure that our laws are sufficiently developed so as to include all members of our family, equally. Because as they say, "charity begins at home." We will persuade the rest of the human race to respect human rights, civil rights, justice and equality when we master these ideals ourselves. We will gain greater respect from the rest of the world when we show that we respect ourselves and our fellow Americans and that true equality exists in our country.

Sandy's spirit still hovers over her beloved country, the United States of America. She hopes that the rights she tried to fight for during her life will continue to be fought for, and ultimately won, by and for others like herself who cared about having an American society where justice is equal and available for all people.

The end.

Some sources used:

- Wikipedia
- https://www.pinterest.com/pin/476326098067050836/
- http://www.cosmopolitan.com/politics/a44215/sandra-bland-sharon-cooper-sister/
- http://www.dailymail.co.uk/video/news/video-1199642/New-video-Sandra-Blands-arrest-later-died-jail.html
- https://www.facebook.com/MyNaturalSistas/videos/1168639983152111/
- http://www.nytimes.com/2015/12/22/us/grand-jury-finds-no-felony-committed-by-jailers-in-

death-of-sandra-bland.html?_r=0

- https://www.youtube.com/watch?v=CaW09Ymr2BA
- Text from various interntional treaties.